A Very Special Gift For You

For:

From:

Norwood is a beautiful writer with the ability to convey volumes in the description of a simple moment.

— *NAPRA Book Review*

THE PATH
OF THE

Wealthy Soul™

by DR. MICHAEL R. NORWOOD

GLOBAL PUBLISHING

Norwood, Michael R.
    The path of the wealthy soul / author: Michael R. Norwood ; editor: Colleen Goidel ; book designer: Rudy Ramos. — 1st ed.
    p. cm. — (The wealthy soul series)
    LCCN 2001-118859
    ISBN 0-911649-06-9

    1. Success. 2. Spiritual life. 1. Title.

BJ1611.2.N67 2001   158.1
                        QB101-701096

Wealthy Soul Books & Movies
Phone: 520-921-0534
Fax: 206-339-6420
E-mail: *publisher@wealthysoul.com*

STUDY GUIDE

The 9 Insights of the Wealthy Soul *(Book 1)*

The Path of the Wealthy Soul *(Book 2)*

The Vision of the Wealthy Soul *(Book 3)*

This is a little book. It's easy and quick to read. Don't confuse the size of it or the simplicity of its message with the profundity of what it can do for you.

Though you can read any of the Wealthy Soul handbooks in just a few hours, the concepts are designed to be read over and over again, one at a time, before you go to bed, when you arise, and as a reminder during the day. Don't stop until they are second nature, until you traverse some of your own great challenges with them ... *until these lessons are ingrained as part of who you are ...*

a Wealthy Soul.

WHO IS A WEALTHY SOUL?

Wealthy Souls are masters of life. They have a certain grace and simplicity yet tremendous underlying power.

They are not easy to recognize. Like a desert blossom, which appears only after a once-a-year rain, their underlying beauty and tenacity may not be apparent at first glance. Sometimes it requires knowing them through the seasons.

So *who* is a Wealthy Soul? Very few souls, indeed.

But who can *become* a Wealthy Soul? Ahhh …

You Can.

Are wealthy people Wealthy Souls?

There are many wealthy people. But money does not make one a Wealthy Soul. Without the wisdom of what makes a Wealthy Soul, material wealth can transform a potential Wealthy Soul into a very poor one.

First, has the material wealth been acquired by means of *"The 9 Insights of the Wealthy Soul*◆ "* beginning with *Insight, Timing,* and *Patience*? And has a win-win situation been established throughout the process – especially a win-win maintenance of beauty and balance in that person's overall life?

Or has the wealth been acquired at all costs, stepping on toes, establishing relationships only for gain, and putting others' lives and one's own life out of balance in the process?

And once the success has been achieved, has it nurtured the qualities of evolving happiness, a more charitable heart and more simplicity of needs?

Or has it fostered a tangled web of needing ever more, trusting no one, and never finding peace?

The bad news is, many wealthy people are not Wealthy Souls.

The good news is, to become a Wealthy Soul …

◆ See *The 9 Insights of the Wealthy Soul* by Dr. Michael R. Norwood.

*It takes but an
instant.*

That sounds good!
How do we start?

The passport to become a Wealthy Soul is obtained the moment of understanding the possibility, followed by the decision to take the journey. The ensuing journey spans a lifetime. It is filled with peaks and valleys, awesome highs and terrifying lows, great beauty yet tremendous adversity.

The Wealthy Soul is not a master at avoiding such adversity. In fact, true mastery can only be tested through the medium of great life challenges. Does the soul emerge scarred and damaged? Or does it emerge – after great upheaval – transformed and triumphant?

Does it emerge a Wealthy Soul?

How do you identify a Wealthy Soul?

You need ask yourself only one question …

Who would I want at my side during my time of greatest adversity?

Wooh.

The Wealthy Soul has probably already been there. He has weathered great storms and radiates the quiet wisdom of resilience, kindness and willingness to help others. He is your greatest friend – though it may take major adversity in your life to find that out.

New Yorkers, Americans and citizens worldwide witnessed a sterling example of this after 9/11. Many heroes rose from the ashes of the New York City attack. Among them was New York City's mayor . . .

Rudy Giuliani

Many people had discounted Giuliani's future just before 9/11 when he withdrew from the New York Senate race after being diagnosed with prostate cancer. This difficult news preceded a painful divorce announcement. But such challenges buttressed Giuliani's natural resolve and fortitude into a rock of stability, grace and strength when his city – and the world – suffered one of the worst traumas in history. The mayor's calmness, presence of mind, and gracious sensitivity will shine as a beacon of light and hope from one of the darkest times of our nation.

Normally, you must look long and hard to find such a person. In fact, very few people fit the Wealthy Soul bill. Yet at the time of your greatest adversity, if you are so fortunate, you needn't look any further.

The Wealthy Soul will find you.

He will find me? How?

Because he is already there. He is the one person that comes to your side unbidden. He is the one person who offers a hand before you have asked for it. He is there for you before you have hit bottom. He is the one who you may have ignored during the good times. The one who you may have actually shunned because frivolousness is not his primary nature. Yet he is the one who materializes when you are at your depths …

Just like an angel.

Wayne Dyer

Everyone knows Wayne Dyer as father of the self-help movement and for his mega-bestselling books and tapes: *The Wisdom of the Ages, Real Magic* and *Your Erroneous Zones*. However, one of his least-known works and the story behind it show, beyond any other image, the true depth of the man.

In 1995, Wayne Dyer read a newspaper article about a mother who had cared for her comatose daughter at home for 25 years, never sleeping more than two hours at a time in order to feed her daughter and check her insulin levels. Dyer was so moved by the story, he sent the mother, Kaye O'Bara, a copy of one of his books, along with a note saying, "You are my hero."

A few months later, Dyer happened to turn on the television and saw Kaye being interviewed on *Inside Edition*. She was holding the book he had sent her, reading the opening line from it: "This is a book about miracles…"

Deeply moved again, feeling, in his own words that, "There was something more in this," Dyer contacted Kaye. He became a regular visitor to her home, bringing his family, sensing an incredible spirituality from the devotion of this woman to her daughter, Edwarda. He eventually wrote a book about the profound nobility of spirit of Kaye and the richness of love and holiness he and his family experienced in her and Edwarda's presence. To this day, all Dyer's royalties from his book *A Promise is a Promise* are donated to help pay for the tremendous medical expenses that were bankrupting Ms. O'Bara.

Though the book never became a mega-bestseller like his other books, it made two lives much easier – and in so doing, Wayne Dyer wrote perhaps his greatest book of all.

The greatest
acts of a
Wealthy Soul
are often the
least counted.

I went through a tremendous adversity.
No one was there for me.

Yes. This is the problem. As I've said, there are very few *true* Wealthy Souls. Very few people who will *truly be there for us* at our time of greatest adversity. Very few people who are strong enough and wise enough – who are *wealthy* enough – to know how or be willing to help a brother or sister in need.

The problem is, our culture has slowly moved us into a stance of competitiveness and *me, myself* and *I* thinking. After 9/11, however, for a long while, many people all over the world went through a personal awakening. A spirit of cooperation and the understanding of *When I extend a hand to you, I open both our hearts* blossoms from such experiences.

Rather than living a contracted, self-absorbed life, the open heart of the Wealthy Soul creates a free-spiritedness that magnetizes people and wealth of every kind. And anyone in business knows that people – *contacts* – are everything.

The old saying, "It's not what you know but who you know," describes this well. But even this adage can use a little fine-tuning with a classic line from a popular 1970s television drama:

It's not who you know;

it's who loves ya, baby!

Meaning ... ?

Meaning that you can know the President of the United States, but if you kicked sand in his face when you were both in high school, you're most likely not going to suddenly find his hand extended to help you one day.

We never know who the "presidents" in our lives are going to be, nor how even the least "flashy" of our acquaintances may one day be the ones who are there for us in our moment of need.

This is not the Wealthy Soul's motivation for helping others. Yet the indescribable joy of living free-spiritedly and with an open heart – along with the huge circle of grateful people that over the years begins to build around the Wealthy Soul – provides him more riches than the material wealth he often achieves.

At the same time, the Wealthy Soul does not spend all his time helping others. You cannot truly help others on a deep level unless you are truly strong yourself. There is a balance to strike. The Wealthy Soul knows when he needs to withdraw his energy to focus on his next step, and when it's appropriate to extend himself out to the world.

Wealthy Souls are like mighty trees. They have strong roots in the ground for their own nourishment, yet beautiful leaves and blossoms to shade and seed others.

What makes such a person?

Adversity is the Wealthy Soul's firebrand.

Wayne Dyer grew up being shuffled from one foster home to another. This was the breeding ground for a heart so noble that, as an adult, he was moved to the point of incredible action after seeing the devotion of a mother to her comatose daughter.

Rather than scarring him, the Wealthy Soul's adversity molds him, providing him an internal scale to measure everything else life can throw at him. He is the tree that has survived the greatest storm. He will survive the next.

He achieves material wealth from his clear-headedness, patience and Vision.* He may even have lost a great fortune, but it is in the recovery that he discovers wealth of many kinds.

Like that mighty tree, his power comes from a combination of strength and flexibility.

The greatest characteristic of the Wealthy Soul is that ...

---

* See *The Vision of the Wealthy Soul* by Dr. Michael R. Norwood.

The Wealthy Soul achieves Balance.

Does the Wealthy Soul have perfect *Balance?*

The Wealthy Soul is not perfect in any way. He makes mistakes.

Frequently.

He is constantly redirecting. Constantly fine-honing his responses. Constantly rebalancing.

*Balance provides
the very roots
of the
Wealthy Soul.*

Explanation, please.

Before a person can be capable of truly helping another or achieving success that truly nourishes himself and those around him, he must achieve a certain balance.

Finding this balance is a daily task, and the Wealthy Soul is ever aware of it. His roots – his balance – have a story we are all aware of: that of being thrown off track and responding to it.

The Wealthy Soul
ever seeks to
re-find The Path.

What do you mean by "The Path" and how does it relate to balance?

The Path is our life's journey. *We choose it.*

Though choosing the path of balance sounds natural, in truth, most of us develop comfort levels with our imbalances, rather than trying to transform them into stepping stones to paths of higher ground. Whether it is sex, food addiction, codependent relationships, or narrow pursuits of money, we accept our imbalances and allow our lives to revolve around them.

With each successive step – or misstep – with each successive imbalance – the Wealthy Soul ever finds higher ground and higher balance.

Balance is the process of constant rebalancing.

Darn, we live in such a crazy world. Besides Wayne Dyer, can you give me an example of just one other person who is balanced?

All Wealthy Souls achieve a high level of balance. But there is another person who truly is a Wealthy Soul in every sense of the word – someone who is truly one of my favorite examples. Someone whom millions of people around the world love, as well.

Bill Cosby

Bill Cosby originally made his name as a comedian, rising to become one of the most successful, wealthy and beloved entertainers of all time. His first starring role was in *I Spy*, a groundbreaking show in that it was the first time an African-American held a lead television role. He later starred in *The Cosby Show*, another groundbreaking show in the way it portrayed an African-American family. Along the way, Cosby wrote several best-selling books including *Childhood* and the mega-hit, *Fatherhood*.

The values Bill Cosby maintained throughout his meteoric rise reflect the highest qualities of a Wealthy Soul. They also provide a model of values for the television industry where such values are often hard to find.

Bill Cosby's appeal is so universal, it's hard to see him as anything but Bill Cosby. Yet as an African-American, he has had to overcome tremendous adversity and prejudice during his rise to fame. As with all true Wealthy Souls, he transcends the categories we habitually put people into.

Rather than make a career out of witty sarcasm and put-downs like so many comedians past and present, Bill Cosby's career was made by the love he felt – and made us feel – for all of humanity. His humor makes his subjects laugh with him rather than cringe with embarrassment from him. It has always raised his audience above all fear, prejudice, and collective insecurity. It lovingly and forgivingly encourages us to look at one another with eyes of acceptance, rather than judgment, and with love and laughter in our hearts for the delightfulness of all our shared idiosyncrasies.

Yes, I have been a great fan of Bill Cosby for decades for exactly those reasons.

It's what makes him so unique. He made the mold, rather than try to fit one.

Bill Cosby's life has been far from all humor, however. Every American felt the heart-wrenching loss he and his wife Camille experienced at the death of his beloved son, Ennis. The senseless murder of this young Wealthy Soul, who was studying to become a special education teacher, shook the world. Everyone waited with bated breath to see how Bill Cosby would emerge from this unspeakable trauma. After a time, who emerged was – Bill Cosby.

Unembittered, his spirit surely shaken but still shining, all there was to see was nobility and grace in his choice to accept what could not be changed, and continue on as one of the world's rare models of a truly balanced Wealthy Soul.

The greatest of Wealthy Souls are fathers and mothers to us all.

Hmm. Even the life of "The Cos" had great ups and downs. Does that mean there is no such thing as perfect balance?

Yes and no. A tightrope walker is always correcting sways to the left and right. It is impossible for him not to be pulled off balance for any length of time. He must constantly readjust back to center. The force of gravity demands this.

The Wealthy Soul, likewise, is constantly subjected to unexpected occurrences, disappointments, and setbacks. Just like all of us, he makes mistakes.

Sometimes he makes major mistakes.

Major mistakes? *The Wealthy Soul???*

Of course. He is only human. His own mistakes provide his greatest lessons.

The Wealthy Soul
looks his mistakes
in the eye, owns
up to them, makes
the appropriate
corrections, then
moves on.

*Do you have any examples of Wealthy Souls who
came back from great mistakes or setbacks?*

Thomas Edison

... the man credited for changing the world most dramatically leading into the twentieth-century. His inventions of the light bulb, the phonograph, the electric power station, the first effective motion-picture camera, and the telegraphic stock ticker changed our lives forever. In the process, Edison almost went bankrupt twice: once in his twenties while inventing the light bulb and later, near age sixty, while working on an unsuccessful iron-ore extracting procedure.

But Edison was used to recovering from failures. After all, tens of thousands of failed experiments led to his single most successful one – the light bulb – which lit up the entire world.

Walt Disney

Everyone knows Walt Disney for Disneyland, the multitude of immortal cartoon characters he created – including Mickey Mouse, Donald Duck, and Goofy – not to mention his hit television show, *The Wonderful World of Disney*, and the animated movies his studio continues to produce that invariably become entertainment blockbusters.

What few know is that Disney started with pennies in the bank and was often near bankruptcy while clawing his way from the ground up. The legacy of his struggles is a man whose vision became part of American culture – and one of history's most successful companies on the New York Stock Exchange.

The only loss
leading to doom
is that of spirit,
not of money.

Commander Scott Waddle

There are much graver mistakes than those leading to loss of money. Commander Scott Waddle was one of the navy's most highly regarded submarine captains. At 41 years old, he was captain of the USS Greenville with a sterling 20-year record and a sparkling future.

His career and that perfect record all came to an abrupt end on February 8, 2001, when his submarine hit a Japanese ship killing nine people, including four teenage boys. An international incident was sparked and Commander Waddle had to face a naval Court of Inquiry.

During the trial, Commander Waddle accepted full responsibility for the accident – despite the fact that the series of events preceding the tragedy was partially the result of an oversight by one of his radar crewmen. "The buck stops with me," Waddle said in an NBC Dateline interview. "If a shipmate makes a mistake, it's my mistake."

Waddle's willingness to own up to the oversights leading to the accident, along with his heart-wrenching anguish he expressed to the victims' families, helped assuage their grief and began to heal the furor created between Japan and the U.S. It also transformed his public persona of a heartless perpetrator to the noblest model of how we all make mistakes we can't undo, yet how we can nevertheless rise up from them.

"I so deeply regret that human errors that I made that day resulted in the tragic loss of life," he said. "At the time I did everything I thought was right. I'm right with God on this … {But} give me the punishment you feel is warranted."

The Navy dismissed him honorably from service. In the tragic loss of life and subsequent loss of his career, Commander Waddle nevertheless rose to become a symbol for us all of something greater than he otherwise ever could have been.

By accepting that none of us is perfect, a Wealthy Soul can forgive himself and others – and move on to achieve extraordinary things.

Sheesh. Do we always have to learn by mistakes and setbacks? Can't our lives be more steady?

Life is always changing … just as the weather and the seasons around a mighty tree are always changing. The only thing any of us can control is *how we change* according to what is changing around us.

Change powers growth. In good times or bad times, the Wealthy Soul is constantly changing, constantly readjusting his timelines, his goals, and where he places his energy.

To live the life of
a Wealthy Soul,
you must always
be changing, too.

Doesn't a Wealthy Soul ever rest?!

Of course. Quiet periods provide the *power* for change. But try to stop change entirely and you stop growth. If you stop growth, you stop *life*. And if you stop life, you stop evolution.

Life is on hold without change.

So how does a Wealthy Soul stay balanced
with all this change?

Paradoxically, by constant periods of quiet. The Wealthy Soul is a *banker* of quiet. Everyday, he takes periods of silence between activities to build up his account of internal quietness. This may be just a minute or two of closing his eyes, listening to music, or going for a brief walk. Rarely does he work pell-mell the whole day through.

He recognizes that …

*The power of
activity is directly
proportional to
the power of
silence.*

In such a busy world, how does he find time *for silence?*

The Wealthy Soul understands that when one has internal quietude, one makes clearer decisions. Our path, our lives, our success and our internal silence are all products of these decisions – not just the major decisions, but the hundreds of tiny decisions we make each day: to walk instead of drive, to smile instead of ignore, to take catnaps instead of drink coffee, to take time instead of rushing, to take a break rather than push on.

Tiny decisions are the molders of destiny.

What is the difference between destiny and fate?

It is the difference between the Wealthy Soul and those souls who are not wealthy. When we make too many unbalancing tiny decisions, ultimately we feel like we have lost control of the big decisions and that life is no longer under our control.

This is fate.

Tell me more.

When we feel at the mercy of fate, we have lost sight of the fact that all we need to do is gain control of those minute-by-minute tiny decisions. The longer we ignore the importance of tiny decisions, the longer it may take us to regain control of the big ones. But slowly, with balanced tiny decisions, the big decisions start returning to our control.

This is Destiny.

That sounds so easy!

To start changing our tiny decisions and become Wealthy Souls of destiny rather than poor creatures of fate ...

We can make the decision to start any time.

Why are decisions so important?

They are the fulcrums of life. Each decision is like a bend in a stream. All streams lead to a river. And all great rivers ultimately lead to the ocean.

The question is, does the stream have the power to reach the river and eventually the ocean? Or will it peter out, an unfulfilled promise?

*Success on all
levels depends on
two things:
One is decisions.
The other is that
which good
decisions are
dependent upon . . .*

Yes?

Decisions are the *directing force* of success. They determine the path of least resistance, the journey that allows a stream to continue using universal forces – gravity, in this case – to reach the ocean.

But there is another factor – the factor that governs all decisions. The *driving force.* Indeed ...

There is
a Power Source.

A Power Source?

No stream can reach a river, and no river an ocean without it. The power source of the stream is *its source*. Does it come from a tiny brook with too little resources to enable its journey? Or does it originate from a mighty reservoir, atop a high mountain, constantly fed by the heavens above?

Is the Power Source connected to the Highest Source?

Della Reese

If ever there was an example of a true Wealthy Soul whose entire life and success was a testimony to being connected to that Power Source, it's Della Reese.

Born in 1931 in the slums of Detroit, Della had every disadvantage imaginable. Poor, black and female, the only thing she had going for her was an indomitable spirit and an astounding voice that transmitted that spirit with the resounding beauty and power of a commandment from God.

In a career with as many lows as highs, Della has had every adversity thrown at her one can imagine. Her mother died when she was in college. Her father couldn't afford the tuition, so she was forced to quit school. She came close to death twice – once in 1970 when she walked through a plate glass door and lost seven pints of blood, and again in 1979, when she collapsed during an appearance on *The Tonight Show* after an aneurysm in her brain ruptured.

Add to that a former husband who beat her, two miscarriages and a protracted battle with the IRS, and it's hard to imagine that this same woman earned her first gold record at age 26 selling over one million copies, had her own TV talk show, is the minister of a standing-room-only church, and starred in the hit television show *Touched by an Angel*.

Now in her early seventies, Della is quick to credit her success and triumph over so much adversity to "an abiding faith that was instilled in me forever." From every song she sings to the angel she plays on television, from her autobiography to the sermons she preaches, that Power Source is her inspiration and her message.

In Della's own words:

"God is consciously aware of you and me and waits for us to turn to him for the abundant life he designed for us.
I believe that,
so I keep turning within to him, which is abundance."

*Hmmm. Getting connected to the Power Source.
I think I'm beginning to see …*

Yes, "see" is the operative word for the Wealthy Soul. "In*sight*" into the nature of life, its source and its flow. And most importantly, to obtain …

Vision.

Vision.

Yes, Vision. Vision, asked for – *prayed for* – from our Creator. The *insight* of where our lives are meant to be directed. What ocean awaits us, its mighty arms beckoning, almost like a father calling … the same Father who sent us on our journey.

The Wealthy Soul has received such Vision.◆ His entire life is empowered by it … despite the many boulders that may block his way. Despite the many streams that may intersect his path, sometimes aligning with him, sometimes seeming to run him off course. But the reservoir of the Wealthy Soul's strength, received by the highest source, empowers every twist and turn to allow him one day to realize his …

◆ See *The Vision of the Wealthy Soul* by Dr. Michael R. Norwood.

VISION:
The quintessential purpose and destination of this lifetime.

And thus … the term "destiny."

Exactly. Just as we have done in our conversation. Returning to destiny. Coming full circle.

The beginning and the end of the Wealthy Soul's journey is his Vision.

*So, does Vision have something to do with how
the Wealthy Soul weathers great storms
and helps others do the same?*

Absolutely. A Wealthy Soul's Vision gives him balance and perseverance. It allows for continued growth through the storms and changing seasons. It allows time for giving of himself, so that he will be given unto. This balance spreads firm roots.

The Wealthy
Soul's Vision
anchors him so
that he may reach
for the sky.

Mikhail Gorbachev

One of the men of greatest Vision in the latter half of the twentieth century – a man who single-handedly did more for world peace and unity than any other of his time literally changing world history and altering the map of the world – is Mikhail Gorbachev.

A soft-spoken man in contrast to the foot-stomping, booming-voiced Russian leaders who preceded him, Gorbachev was described by the foreign minister who helped bring him to power as "the man with the nice smile" but who has "iron teeth."

From the first day of his entry into power, those iron teeth would shred the old bureaucracy that had defined the Soviet Union for decades. He immediately cracked down on corruption and drunkenness and soon instituted *glasnost*, which allowed for unprecedented public review and monitoring of the government as well as publication of previously banned literary works, such as *Dr. Zhivago*. He encouraged modernization, openness and democratization of every level of Russian society. His actions ultimately led to the dissolution of the Soviet Union, the fall of the Berlin Wall, and the end of an era in which world superpowers could at any moment create nuclear war and annihilation.

Because of the turmoil that follows all great change, Gorbachev stepped down from his position in 1991. But his creation of a more united, safer and democratic world continues today as a direct result of his actions and Vision.

What he accomplished now seems more an act of God than one of probability, and can probably best be explained by understanding that …

People of Vision are tools of God.

Yes, but Gorbachev lost it all in the process.

Indeed, he sacrificed his personal gain for that of his country and the world. But his willingness to do so – his understanding that the price of his undertakings might ultimately be sacrificing his position and power – was a decision he made the moment he decided to honor his Vision.

Gorbachev's decision, as well as his Vision, were certainly cultivated over years, modified by the rapidly changing times of that era, yet slowly crafted into fine-honed actions that ultimately remodeled the world.

OK. So, back to decisions … little ones and big ones. How do you make good ones?

The good ones are aligned with your Vision. They have a "sense of rightness" to them. They sometimes fly in the face of logic. They are often unconventional. Who among the Soviet leadership would have supported Gorbachev's rise to power had they seen what he had envisioned?

People who do not have the Wealthy Soul's Vision do not understand the decisions a Wealthy Soul makes.

Be directed by your Vision – not by such people.

Uh, can we hold on here just a minute?
This sounds awfully important ...

This *is* important. If you pardon the expression ...

Your fate
— or your destiny —
is held in the
balance.

Yes ... hmm. Maybe we should ... uh ... just back up a little here? Can you explain more about making good decisions?

Good decisions *feel* more comfortable. Until we cultivate what that subtle sense "feels" like, it may be difficult at the moment of the decision to know if that decision is good or not.

For instance, if you are in the presence of a skilled con artist, he may have you believing everything he says. If you "sign on the dotted line" at that moment, you will soon learn what the contrasting feeling of *discomfort* is – in the harshest way.

However, if you resist temptation and consider how you feel in quiet reflection – away from this person's influence – you'll see that something "just doesn't feel right" about him and his "deal."

To cultivate that sense of comfort vs. discomfort, avoid making snap decisions. And ...

When uncertain,
don't choose
"yes" or "no."
Choose reflection.

*Is there any way to know – at the moment – if a
decision is good or bad?*

The more you practice reflecting and the more conscious
you become, the easier it becomes to "feel" that sense of rightness
immediately. Proposals by con artists will be much easier to recognize after awhile. And more importantly, the *next steps* on your
life path will be illuminated with greater certainty.

It's the little decisions – which usually aren't completely good
or bad, but rather "more good" or "less good" – that require
greater skill.

It takes practice to cultivate that "feeling" of what a comfortable decision is.

Which leads to the question:
What exactly is that "feeling?"

Decisions that are not in line with our path and our destiny create a subtle *charge* inside us. To feel that charge, we can't be *overcharged* to begin with.

Good little decisions prevent us from being overcharged so that we can feel the "comfort" of good bigger decisions.

What do you mean by "a charge?"

Electrical activity. The number of neurons that are firing at once inside our brains and bodies. Too many and we feel rushed, hyper, "wired."

Too few and we feel bored, tired, "no spark."

Occasionally it is good to feel "charged." We break a rule and we break a boundary. We feel *alive!*

But if you live that way regularly – on the wild side – see how quickly life becomes out of balance.

Rules serve a purpose. Yet all rules are meant to eventually be broken … but over time and with understanding.

The key to balance
is to have a spark
but not be wired.

Can you give an example?

Sure. Say you're playing chess with a friend. Your child comes in and turns on the television. Another child comes in complaining he's hungry, when will dinner be ready? Suddenly you're no longer playing chess. You might as well just pack up and prepare dinner.

*Being overcharged
is often a product
of trying to do
too many things
at once.*

So, what you're saying is – to prevent being over-charged, you must be focused.

Precisely!

Your degree of focus will determine your degree of effectiveness.

Is focus the only factor to prevent becoming overcharged?

No. Too much focus and you can't change. Skilled con artists accomplish their enticement by focusing their prey so completely that they lose their rationality ... along with their money.

Or, when playing chess, if you block out your child completely, the child will go hungry. Having to deal later with a hungry, irritable child will equally overcharge you.

On a larger scale, many people have focused on their goals to the exclusion of all else and all others in their lives. Though they often achieve great material success and even high-profile recognition, they are not Wealthy Souls. They are people who usually have great marital distress, unruly children, and unhealthy bodies.

A key to becoming a Wealthy Soul is the ability to change direction ...to develop "Flexible Focus."

Roma Downey

What better example of this quality of a Wealthy Soul than seeing it in an angel? One who is companion in both real-life and television to another angel: namely Della Reese, who was portrayed previously.

In the hit television show *Touched by an Angel*, Roma Downey starred as Monica, a loveable human-form messenger of God who in each episode, with a beguiling mixture of whimsicality and grace, helped transform the lives of ordinary people into those of Wealthy Souls.

Yet Roma's real life was not all whimsicality and charm. Born in war-torn Northern Ireland, she grew up amid gunfire, bombs and the killing of people she knew. When Roma was 10, she witnessed her mother's death from a heart attack. "Her death left a big hole that I grew up around," Roma shares. "There was always a feeling of emptiness in my life."

In 1996, the birth of her daughter, Reilly Marie, filled the gap in her heart, but her marriage to Reilly's father ended several years later. "It's a big responsibility when you have a career and a wee one," Roma said in an interview. "It's even harder when you have to do it alone."

But Roma does it gracefully, bringing her daughter to filming sites for at least half the day, having lunch with her and playing with her between scenes. Roma's achievement of balancing a demanding career, stardom and parenthood well illustrates the meaning of Flexible Focus.

Even without knowing this, millions of souls have been touched by something that seems to come from deep within the actress's own soul – Flexible Focus being only one of the resulting attributes. Anyone who ever watched the show can sense a depth and a grace that transcends mere acting gifts. It is something you see only in one who has passed through great trials. And even then, so rarely.

As rare as a Wealthy Soul.

So Flexible Focus is an important attribute.
How does one develop it?

Back to taking breaks – as Roma Downey does with her daughter; by just accepting that we have to fit something else in our lives besides a single-tracked focus.

And when we're alone, we maintain Flexible Focus by having moments of quiet – reconnecting with the silent source of our Vision.

When we take regular breaks, if our activity is interrupted, it becomes just another break.

To summarize ...

The key to maintaining balance is to take breaks and maintain Flexible Focus.

So how do you put this whole thing together, this subject of decisions?

Big decisions are like a ship's rudder, little ones are like its ballast. In other words, in a Wealthy Soul's life ...

The purpose of big decisions is direction. The purpose of little ones is balance.

So, in other words, a boat may reach its destination without balance and ballast, but it will be a mighty rough journey?

It may *sink* in the process. Which leads us to our next subject:

Intersecting paths

Intersecting paths? Enlighten me.

The shortest distance between two points is a straight line. The shortest distance between where we are now and where our Vision leads us *is not a straight line.* It's *life* itself. And it ain't straight! Many other paths will intersect ours:

> A complementary soul to unite with us as
>   husband or wife
> A child to be born
> A stranger's request for directions
> A friend's need for a hand
> A parent's need for our love
> Roses to smell along the way
> Birthdays to celebrate
> Deaths to grieve
> Wounds to heal
> Wrongs to be righted
> Adversities to triumph over ...

As long as we slowly and consistently work toward our Vision, every event – however distracting it seems from our path – in truth, is just a reminder:

*Vision is a
lifelong process.
It's what happens
<u>on the way</u>
that makes us
Wealthy Souls.*

The Dalai Lama

There is no greater example of dealing with an unrelenting Intersecting Path than the life of The Dalai Lama. In 1937, at age 2, he was chosen as the next leader of Tibet. When he was 15, China invaded his country, intersecting his path and changing his life and that of his countrymen forever. Brutal tactics were used to repress resistance; in the ensuing years, tens of thousands of his countrymen were murdered and many more mercilessly tortured.

In 1959, the Dalai Lama had to flee his own country to escape imprisonment. At age 19, he began negotiating for the fate of Tibet with Chinese leader Mao Tse-tung. To this day, in exile, he continues the battle for his country. But that battle is an inner one as much as a political one – and by his own example and teachings, though he has not yet won his country back, the Dalai Lama has won the respect and love of an entire world.

In describing his fight for his country, he says, "The antidote to hatred in the heart – the source of violence – is tolerance. You could call this practice *inner disarmament*. We also call it *the best armor* since it protects you from being conquered by hatred."

To this day, the Dalai Lama is a leader without a country. Yet via his method of accepting the Intersecting Path that forever changed his destiny, he has become a spiritual leader for the entire world.

"When we meet real tragedy, we can react in two ways: either by losing hope and falling into self-destructive habits … or by using the challenge to find our inner strength."

– The Dalai Lama

Beth & Rob Stein

I first met Beth Stein in Atlanta, Georgia, where she was struggling to eke out a living as a computer consultant for private individuals and small businesses. She became a good friend after setting me up on my first notebook computer.

A year after I met her, Beth married her long-time sweetheart, Rob, and moved to Cincinnati, Ohio. I lost track of them for three years. Then one day, while flipping through my phone book, I came across their number and called to say hello. To my amazement, Beth told me how she and Rob had started a software duplication company, and in a few short years, had built it into an organization of 25 employees, housed in a 15,000 square foot office, and valued at four million dollars. I was both shocked and thrilled for them. Though we spoke only sporadically, I enjoyed hearing about the continuation of their phenomenal success.

Then two years went by before I spoke to Beth and Rob again. This time, however, the story had changed quite dramatically. With the Year 2000 crash of the dot.com industry, a key investor pulled out of their business and sales dropped 70 percent. Having come from nothing, Beth and Rob knew they had the internal fortitude to survive. But it would require incredible fighting with all the resources they had. Then Beth became unexpectedly pregnant. To further complicate matters, she was pregnant with triplets. Two embryos died in a rare syndrome called "Vanishing Twins." The single surviving embryo was struggling and Beth was severely bleeding. She and Rob were forced to choose: sacrifice their business by stopping their fight for it, or continue fighting and possibly lose their unborn child.

They opted for the former, declaring bankruptcy and dissolving the company. Today, when I speak to Beth and Rob, though there is still great anguish over the loss of their material wealth and hard-fought empire, they have no regrets over the decision that gifted them with a beautiful, now healthy child.

*When we resist
an intersecting
path, we lose the
direction God is
lovingly pointing
us and forfeit
that opportunity
to become a
Wealthy Soul.*

How is it possible to stay focused?
There are so many things that happen in our lives.

The 9 Insights of the Wealthy Soul⁕ provide the answer –
particularly the first four: **Insight, Timing, Patience** and
Surrender.

Insight provides us with our Vision.

Timing is how we recognize when the events of the world –
the intersecting paths – line up in space and time to allow us to
take our next step.

Patience provides our ability to wait for the arrival of a high
point of energy in the cycle – the best next step.

And **Surrender** …

⁕ See *The 9 Insights of the Wealthy Soul* by Dr. Michael R. Norwood.

Surrender turns the process over to God.

*To achieve a Vision it seems you have to
spend lots of time passing time.*

The fifth and sixth insight – **Grounding** and **Balance** –
provide for this paradox:

Grounding keeps us in touch with our Vision and our life.

Balance enables us to heed which of the two is calling most
at the moment.

The interchange of our life and our Vision is the cycle that powers a Wealthy Soul forward.

Isn't a lifetime a long time to wait for our Vision to come to fruition? Isn't there a quicker way?

The last three Insights answer that question. **Growth, Evolution** and **Transformation.**

Growth occurs in direct proportion to the lessons we learn while balancing the interchange of our life and our Vision.

Evolution blossoms when our growth takes us to a new and higher stage of life, unfolding *a vision of our Vision* even we never foresaw!

Transformation is the final stage of our evolution as Wealthy Souls, when Vision and life become one. We then see that each moment of our life, like a hologram, contained the lessons of the entire journey ... our life and our Vision always having been as intertwined as our bodies and souls.

In the end, we as Wealthy Souls understand that our Vision was naught but the map for our life itself.

Now that you're done with this Wealthy Soul handbook, it's a good idea to give yourself a break to let its overall message sink in. After a day or so, read the book again very slowly, concept by concept, biographical portrait by portrait, over a period of one to two weeks. Then, each day for the next 6 to 12 months, randomly flip open to any page and see which insight rings true to what you are supposed to be reminded of that day.

Whenever you feel comfortable, begin another *Wealthy Soul* handbook. A number are already written and many more are coming. Each is designed to add concepts that you'll begin to cultivate on your path as a Wealthy Soul.

At some point, you will want to read **The 9 Insights of the Wealthy Soul,** Michael Norwood's personal story and the book that sparked the entire *Wealthy Soul* series. It is a story of a former WWII pilot nicknamed *The Death-Cheater* – Michael's father – who teaches Michael nine universal principles of transforming rocks into diamonds, imminent crashes into soaring flights, and our greatest life challenges into the highest wealth of the soul.

Each subsequent handbook is designed to show a different facet of that rock-turned-diamond so that …

Any person can transform into a Wealthy Soul — that which we all, on our deepest level, desire to be.

The author in one of his offices.

Michael Norwood is a Doctor of Chiropractic and a board certified kinesiologist and nutritionist with extensive post-graduate training in neurology and holistic medicine. The *Wealthy Soul* series has roots in his childhood, growing up with a sibling who suffered from terminal cancer. The beautiful gifts and grace he received through that experience were crystallized by his father, a former WWII pilot nicknamed *The Death-Cheater*, who taught him *The 9 Insights of the Wealthy Soul* — lessons about transforming adversity into wealth of every kind. His father was battling his own illness at the time.

Michael recently moved to the red rock canyon country of Sedona, Arizona where he teaches seminars and writes *Wealthy Soul* books from various prime office locations.

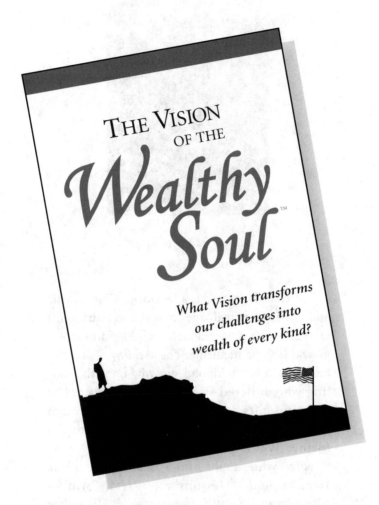

The Vision that changes your life . . .

and simultaneously begins changing the lives of those around you is possible for everyone. Such Vision lifts us up from life's greatest challenges, gives power and purpose to our every day, and often results in great material wealth. This book is about those who have it, what enables you to receive it, and how such Vision will transform all your adversity into the greatest wealth of the soul

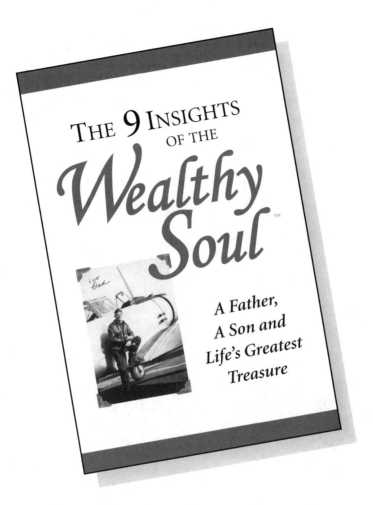

THE **9** INSIGHTS
OF THE

Wealthy Soul™

A Father,
A Son and
Life's Greatest
Treasure

"Destined to be a classic."
—ROSANNE WELCH
Producer of ***Touched by an Angel***

A former WWII pilot — battling a grave illness — teaches his son
9 unforgettable lessons about transforming all our adversities,
setbacks and losses into wealth of every kind.

RECEIVE YOUR *FREE* BONUS GIFTS
at www.wealthysoul.com,
Michael's thanks for having obtained his books:

FREE - Michael's online Wealthy Soul Newsletter. Filled with action steps and stories that will begin transforming all your challenges into wealth of every kind.

FREE inspirational Flash movie presentations of Michael's *30 Gifts of Life* poems. The movies of the poems took Michael 3 years to produce. The links to view them will be emailed to you one per week for 30 weeks. The movies will continually inspire you to discover the greatest wealth in your own life.

FREE audios, radio and television shows, and upcoming teleconferences with Michael. Subjects include Michael's newest revelations about *The 30 Gifts of Life* and *The 9 Insights of the Wealthy Soul*. Continue discovering these exquisite Gifts and Insights everyday on your own path.

Sign up to receive your free gifts at
www.wealthysoul.com

ORDER FORM

 # Qty:

_____ The 9 Insights of the Wealthy Soul @ $19.95 $_____

_____ The Path of the Wealthy Soul @ $14.95 $_____

_____ The Vision of the Wealthy Soul @ $14.95 $_____

Wealthy Soul Gift Pack (all 3 items above) @ **$29.95** (40% off)

# of Gift Packs:_____ x **$29.95** = $ _____

Subtotal : $_____

SHIPPING & HANDLING:
U.S.: add $8.95 for 1-3 books,
and $1 for each additional book. $_____

Canada: $16.95 for 1-3 books
$2 for each additional book. $_____

All other countries: $29.95 (Global Express) for 1-3 books
$3 for each additional book. $_____

Arizona Residents: add sales tax
per the county you live in. $_____

TOTAL AMOUNT FOR ORDER $.

Telephone Orders: **888-822-4694;** Fax Orders: **206-339-6420**
Web orders: **www.wealthysoul.com**

Mail Orders: Wealthy Soul, 65 Verde Valley School Rd, Suite H13, Sedona, AZ 86351

Name: _____

Address: _____

City:_____ State: _____ Zip: _____

Country:_____ E-mail address: _____

Payment: ☐ Check   ☐ VISA   ☐ MasterCard   ☐ Discover Card   ☐ AMEX

Card #:_____ Expires: _____

RECEIVE YOUR *FREE* BONUS GIFTS

at www.wealthysoul.com,
Michael's thanks for having obtained his books:

FREE - Michael's online Wealthy Soul Newsletter. Filled with action steps and stories that will begin transforming all your challenges into wealth of every kind.

FREE inspirational Flash movie presentations of Michael's *30 Gifts of Life* poems. The movies of the poems took Michael 3 years to produce. The links to view them will be emailed to you one per week for 30 weeks. The movies will continually inspire you to discover the greatest wealth in your own life.

FREE audios, radio and television shows, and upcoming teleconferences with Michael. Subjects include Michael's newest revelations about *The 30 Gifts of Life* and *The 9 Insights of the Wealthy Soul.* Continue discovering these exquisite Gifts and Insights everyday on your own path.

Sign up to receive your free gifts at
www.wealthysoul.com